I Think,
Therefore IB

I Think, Therefore IB

The Ultimate Guide to Survival and
Success in the IB Diploma Program

ALEXANDER ZOUEV

ZOUEV PUBLISHING

Published 2011
Printed by Lightning Source

ISBN 978-0-9560873-2-4, paperback.

Dedicated to all those who never believed in me

TABLE OF CONTENTS

INTRODUCTION..1

IB FEAR 8

SUBJECT CHOICE..11

A DAY IN THE LIFE OF IB 24

INTERNAL ASSESSMENT 33

CAS 43

REVISION 51

STRESS MANAGEMENT 68

PAST PAPERS..72

EXAMINATION TECHNIQUE 84

APPEALS/RETAKES 95

ACADEMIC DISHONESTY...99

INTRODUCTION

Congratulations on obtaining the easiest, cheapest and most efficient method of earning a 40+ grade on your International Baccalaureate Diploma. Whether you are a student in need of guidance, a teacher looking to find new teaching techniques, or simply an interested reader – hopefully you will find that this short but to-the-point book meets all of your expectations.

Before diving into the world I like to call "stress-free IB" you may want to ask yourself the question "why should I to listen to some stranger's advice on how to do well on my IB?" At least I hope you are asking yourself this question. After all, I have never taught the IB, nor am I in any way affiliated with the organisation or have any sort of teaching degree. Moreover, in recent years the market for IB 'help' material has become greatly saturated with both recommendable and also some avoidable books being published. Thus, before going into the details of how to maximize your IB points total, let me put your mind at ease by providing a little background on myself and my own academic experiences.

Having completed my IB diploma in 2007 with an overall score of 43, I went on to read Economics and Management at Oxford University, from where I most recently graduated. At this point, some of you may begin to ask whether it would make more sense to obtain advice from someone who has gotten a 45 on their IB, or better yet a qualified IB teacher who has decades of experience teaching the program. The answer is very simple. I know exactly how it feels to be an average student struggling with the program, looking for all the right resources and answers with minimal effort. The student that gets 45 will most of the time be someone who has great natural intelligence, but probably devoted most of his/her teenage years to the books rather than living a normal teen life. In other words it's not me or you. What I can offer you is fool-proof advice and techniques on how to obtain 7's in most of your subjects without having to work relentlessly and waste countless hours staying up and memorizing useless information.

In truth, I am the type of person that does not like to miss a party. I can recall that five weeks before the start of exams some of my friends and I went clubbing on Friday, Saturday and Sunday only to have to sit mocks the following week. Having a mind-blowing hangover the size of

Ireland's debt on the morning of Senior Day, three weeks before exams, is another fond memory. The point is that you need not drop all your social gatherings, athletic events and personal hobbies in order to survive in the world of IB. In fact, you don't need to drop any. Some of the most successful IB candidates I know were all captains of a sports team, busy jumping from one relationship to another, or recovering every other Saturday morning from excessive drinking. Their secret? Natural intelligence? Perhaps. But in most of the cases it was simply an ability to be efficient, hard-working when necessary, and only doing what was essential in order to get the grade they need. No more, no less. All of these tips you can expect to find in this book.

If you follow the advice put forth in this book correctly and put in some effort and determination, I firmly believe that you can obtain a points total of 40 or above – irrespective of any 'natural' intelligence. If, however, you are someone less ambitious, looking to score 7's in some of your subjects whilst maintaining a pass in others, then you will simply need to flip to the chapters that suit your needs. The subtitle of the book does mention both the words 'success' and 'survival', which may seem a contradiction at first, but to me it merely highlights the dual effectiveness of the book's advice. If you are someone who has been advised not to do the IB because it is too demanding and are predicted to fail miserably, perhaps this book may indeed become your new survival guide.

Those of you still curious to know, the two points I missed out on to get a 45 where due to a 6 in Physics (Standard Level) and a 6 in English (Standard Level). Looking back I do blame myself for not following my own advice enough to get that 7 in Physics, however the English I have no regrets about; I tried my best and did what I could, but did not get a 7. Unfortunately, this book will not teach you how to get a perfect score of 45/45 and place you into the top 0.01% of candidates. I know plenty of people who have obtained this amazing feat; however, almost all admit to having had a slice of good fortune somewhere along their path to perfection. With most university offers capped at around 40 points there is also no need to get a perfect score - unless you are the ultimate perfectionist.

No matter how little natural academic ability you have, I firmly believe that with minimal effort on your part, you simply cannot fail if you read and use this book. There is no effortless way to achieve the grades that you want. There are, however, ways that will save you time, effort and money - yet still let you reach your maximum potential and get the grades of your dreams.

For those of you reading to find any tips on plagiarism, cheating or any other non-ethical method to get a higher grade. You will have to look elsewhere. My tips and techniques are 100% in line with the rules and regulations of the IB guidelines. Understandably, there will be critics amongst parents and teachers who suggest that a lot of what I endorse is in some ways non-ethical and not in accordance with what the IB preaches. These arguments lack merit. Countless students are getting the top grades and succeeding without actually succumbing to becoming lifeless bookworms. One needs to understand and appreciate that there is "cheating" and then there are "tactical and efficient study techniques", and there is a thick line separating the two concepts. This book will ultimately teach you to become masters of manipulating the resources at your disposal efficiently and tactically, without having to resort to anything that can be regarded as 'cheating'.

What is essential, before we begin, is that you throw away all preconceived notions about the IB as being something scary, elitist, incredibly demanding and impossible to crack. I was once amongst you, but after finding out that the IB is just as easy to decipher as the A-levels, the AP programs, or the SATs – I became fearless. This is an essential stepping-stone in your long road to IB success. Yes, your non-IB friends will call you an overachieving geek. Yes, you may find you have more assignments and tests than the other "normal" kids. And yes, there will be times when you wonder why your parents/teachers would ever want to put you through so much traumatising pain. However one should not fear. The techniques in this book will ensure that your two-year ride will be amongst the most memorable and fun two years of your life. It was certainly for me.

Some of you may ask why I didn't produce a book outlining the techniques and methods of success in subjects I myself actually studied (HL: Economics, Mathematics, Geography, SL: English, Dutch, Physics) rather than making an entire manual outlining all the various subjects in less detail. The truth is that most of the techniques I use overlap from subject to subject. Hence, I am able to offer a greater variety of advice to students not necessarily taking those subjects, but still struggling with similar problems. This way the book can offer advice on issues that other more specialized IB books cannot. Namely: study advice, internal assessment advice, past paper advice, and general IB work advice. I will admit that the sections on the subjects that I actually took are more detailed than others, but this should not dissuade you from reading those sections. For example, most of the advice I give on succeeding in HL Mathematics could easily be transferred to those taking SL Mathematics.

The second reason I tried to avoid being too detailed on the specifics of the course is simply because there is already an abundance of good information out there. Although I could spend chapters discussing the detailed syllabus of the IB Economics course, it would be a wasted effort as there are a handful of brilliantly written textbooks on the matter already. What is missing, however, is general advice that applies across subjects and helps you become an efficient and well-rounded IB student. This book aims to fill that void.

IB FEAR

Perhaps the first and most important topic to address is this widespread belief of the IB programme being elitist, unrealistically difficult, and a two year burden on your teenage life. You need to throw away all of your negative preconceptions and fears about the IB diploma and start believing in yourself. No matter who you are and what kind of academic record you have had up to this point in your life, the IB diploma program is an opportunity for you to start anew.

I have known students that have come from C grade averages to end up with high 30s on their IB diploma. I myself was quite the high-school slacker and troublemaker until I realised that my IB grades could decide a large part of my near future. The key here is that natural intelligence and 'smartness' are not essential to achieving IB success. What is essential however is the willpower and self-belief that you can survive and succeed in the most academically intense high school degree program and come out with flying colours.

Consider your two-year IB experience as something of a sporting event. The final exams are the grand finale, and everything before is your preparation and training for that event. I use this sporting analogy because it highlights the importance of planning and mental preparedness that is needed in order to perform at the highest level. Even the greatest athletes cannot do their best unless they master the skill of visualizing their own success.

Without getting too philosophical, I do want to stress how important this 'visualization' exercise is. Unless you can actually imagine yourself getting the top marks and achieving a total of 40+ points, it will be very difficult to do so in reality. This is not a 'self-help' book per se, nor do I fully agree with the ideas that some self-help books tend to promote – most famously *The Secret's* notion that anything is possible if you keep thinking about it. However, although I don't think that visualization alone is sufficient for success, I do think that it is necessary.

When you hear someone tell you that the IB program is 'difficult', you need to appreciate that difficulty is always relative. Yes, perhaps compared to the A-Levels, the IB is more academically challenging and there is more work to be done. However, this does not mean that the IB is the hardest task any 16-18 year olds across the world have to face. Trust me, there will be much more demanding and stressful challenges as you get older. Don't let this 'IB fear' become a scapegoat for underperformance. I see this happen all the time. Students get lost in this illusion of the IB as something impossible, and subsequently lose any motivation to do well because they think it is beyond their reach. This is where mental strength is of upmost importance.

The first few weeks of the IB program are relatively tranquil. Use this 'easing-in' period as an opportunity to prove to yourself that you can conquer and beat anything the IB program throws at you. Only once you overcome your mental fear of the IB program can you begin to deal with the challenges of the program itself. It is imperative that your first few weeks of the program go as smooth as possible. If you start to fall behind early, any preconceived fears you may have had will soon turn into a reality. So at least for the first month or so make sure you meet all of the deadlines and perform at your highest level. Once you have proven to yourself that you can overcome the first month, any fear left will gradually dissolve.

SUBJECT CHOICE

Although to most of you this chapter will have little relevance, to those who are yet to decide which subjects you want to take this chapter is of great importance. I find that choosing your subjects is (unfortunately) underestimated in importance. You are deciding what you will learn in depth for the next two years of your life. So, just as you would take time to choose a college degree, an occupation or a spouse, you should sit down and really think about what interests you - even slightly! There are a few factors that you should take into account and I have outlined these below:

1) Interest

With almost everything you do, you will tend to succeed more and find it easier if you are doing something you actually have an interest for and enjoy. The same goes for IB subjects. Although this is of less importance in choosing a group 1 or 2 language, it has great importance in choosing your group 4 science and group 3 subject. If you know for a fact that you have absolutely no passion and interest for memorizing human anatomy and studying biology, then you can cross that off. If, on the other hand, you want your IB to have as little maths as possible, then you probably would not be too interested in studying Physics. If you are are strongly passionate about a certain subject and are already reading external material concerned with it, then by all means go ahead and take it.

However, one should be careful not to confuse interest with vague curiosity. If you always thought that graffiti is pretty cool, it would not be a wise choice choosing HL Art solely based on that observation. Similarly, don't let a childhood obsession with spaceships be the deciding factor for choosing HL Physics. This is where a slight familiarity with the course content can greatly help. Take the time to glance over the syllabus of the course you are interested in, and only then check to see if it matches your interests.

2) Ability

Obviously if you are clearly naturally gifted in a certain subject then you should thank your natural abilities and take it. Of course there are limitations to this rule of thumb. I used to be obsessed with drawing and graphic design, and for many years believed I would be studying Art at Diploma level. However, as the time came for me to make my final decision, I did a little research (with the statistics that the IB provides on their webpage) and talked to a many seniors who had previously done Art as a subject. The general feeling seemed to be that if I wanted to go for a subject that I enjoyed, excelled at, and wouldn't be under too much stress then I should choose Art instead of another Group 3 topic. Having done that research also showed me that it seemed very few get 7s in Art, no matter how passionate or how good the candidate is (perhaps due to the nature of the final exam and luck of the draw).

Since I was more concerned with obtaining a 7 than following my passion for Art and gambling with the grade, I chose geography (which I also had a reasonable ability for). The message I'm sending here is that often students get confused about how great their abilities are in a certain subject. Just because you got A's in English in Elementary School does not mean that you should expect to jump into a Higher Level English exam and effortlessly produce a grade 7 piece of work. Be honest with yourself when assessing your own ability in a certain subject.

3) Future

Please don't get me wrong. When I say future I don't mean that the subjects you choose for your IB diploma will reflect in any way where you will be in ten years and what sort of occupation you will have. Nevertheless, you do need to take into consideration what you want to do at university level (if you plan on pursuing a university education). It's really unfortunate that you need to be thinking about your post-school decision from almost the age of 16 (when university is probably the last thing on your mind) but that's the reality of it. Too often I have seen students wanting to study medicine at a top UK university be rejected because, despite taking Biology as a subject, they did not take Chemistry (which is often a requirement to study medical science). The same can be said for students wanting to study Economics. Taking Mathematics Studies severely limits your chances of ending up a at a top Economics course - in most cases.

So, if you're one of those students that has his/her heart set on a specific course at a specific university by the age of 16, then you should definitely do some research and find out which courses are essential, and which will help you in getting closer to your goal. For those of you thinking of studying abroad, you may want to reconsider which foreign languages you want to take – if your school offers a wider variety.

Although this is important to take into consideration, don't worry too much about it. In most cases offers from universities are given based on a final score, rather than subject specific. Also, I have seen people go on to get PhD's in Economics without having taken Economics as an IB subject. So, with regards to the long term future, subject choice is probably not the most important factor to consider.

4) Teachers

Tough one. I hate to say it but there is such a thing as a "crap teacher" even in the glamorous top-of-the-line world of the IB Diploma. Trust me; I have seen the best of both worlds. Some of the teachers I have worked with were masters of what they did, with more than a decade of first-hand IB experience. Then there were those who probably couldn't spell International Baccalaureate – let alone teach it. Most students tend to believe this idea where the teacher is the one factor that will make or break the subject. They think that the teacher has a greater influence on the final grade than they themselves do.

I do not agree. Even if your teacher is utterly useless at what they are hired to do, this does not mean you should spend two years moaning only to ultimately fail the subject and live your whole life cursing that teacher. Believe me; I have seen some of the worst of the worst. But even despite the poor teaching I've seen students get past that and take matters into their own hands to come out with a grade they truly deserve. Yes, it's true; if you have a poor teacher then you will spend most of your time becoming best friends with the subject textbooks. But let's be honest here, we don't live in a perfect world, hence we don't all have world class IB teachers.

With regards to the subject material, you should not have to worry too much if your teacher is clueless. But, when it comes to things such as external assessments and choosing options for examinations, you should ensure that they know what they are talking about. You don't want to sit a two year program only to find that your teacher messed up the internal assessments you gave in and as a result you lose almost 25% of your total mark.

By the time you begin your IB program, you will have heard all the rumours about who is a great IB teacher and who shouldn't even be teaching preschool. Don't completely ignore these. If you're the type of person who simply cannot take matters into their own hands and work independently for most of the year, then by all means look for the "best" and most engaging teachers that are available. If, on the other hand, you don't need to be spoon-fed information that is readily available for you yourself to read from the textbooks, then it shouldn't matter. In this case you should choose subjects based on the other criteria I have outlined.

5) School records

If you are one of those students sitting the IB diploma simply to obtain the highest score possible (no matter which subjects) then you would be wise to do a little bit of research. Find out how well your school has performed in different subjects over the years. If for the past ten years, not a single person has gotten a 7 in Chemistry, then your best bet would probably be not to choose it if you are looking for a 7 in your Group 4 subject. If on the other hand, it has been decades since someone has gotten below a 5 in your school's History SL program, and you are the type of person that would be more than happy with a 5 or above then by all means go for it.

Don't limit this research to your school records alone. Go online and find out which subjects have the greatest fail rates, the greatest number of 7's, and what the median marks are. All of this information as readily available on the IBO website – under the section of 'Statistical Bulletins'. There is an abundance of information in these reports, so take the time to really analyse them. I don't encourage making decisions completely based on statistics, but playing the numbers game will not prevent you from making better choices.

6) Difficulty

There is a myth in the IB world that claims that all IB kids do an equal amount of work, no matter what subjects they choose. Perhaps the phrasing is a bit unclear there. Yes, it can be that the actual amount of work (hours assigned) is the same from student to student. Don't be fooled into thinking that each candidate faces the same difficulty. This is especially true because of the IB's system of separating Higher Level and Standard Level subjects.

Take two random students with exactly same subject choices, apart from the fact that student X takes Maths HL and Geography SL, whereas student Y takes Maths Studies (SL) and

Geography HL. One would have an incredibly difficult time arguing that the gap in difficulty between Maths SL and HL is the same as the gap between Geography SL and HL. The gap in difficulty between Maths HL and SL is incomparable to the gap in Geography.

There is no point in kidding ourselves. If you want to challenge yourself, then by all means take HL: Economics, Mathematics, English, Physics, SL: History, 2nd Language. If you want to lay back a bit and not be under too much stress and get a guaranteed pass, take HL: Theatre Arts, Geography, Environmental Systems, SL: English, Language (ab initio), and Business Management. Let's be honest here; it's no secret that Physics, Chemistry or Biology are more demanding than Environmental Systems.

All of this is not something to be ashamed of either. You may opt to take a less stressful route, with a lighter workload – and this is perfectly fine. The point I am trying to make is that you need to figure out what your ultimate aim is. Do you want to choose demanding courses that interest you and will challenge you? Or do not have little interest in what subjects you actually do as long as you get 35+ by the end of the two years? There is little wrong with either of the choices, but the important thing to remember is that the choice is real and the choice is yours.

7) Resources:

As much as the IB tries to make their students more educated, inquisitive and imaginative, I am often shocked at how little students use the resources available at their disposal. The internet is an invaluable weapon in your IB survival toolkit. Go online and find out if there are any great books available on your subjects of interest. Find out how long the course has been taught and whether it has been significantly modified in recent years.

Keep in mind that if the resources are scarce for you subject of interest, then it probably means that you will struggle to find help outside your classroom. More well-established subjects have an incredible surplus of information readily available to find on the internet and in books. The newer subjects, or the less popular choices, will undoubtedly have less helpful information.

Concluding remarks

On a final note, I fully appreciate that there are many students out there crying "my school just launched the IB Diploma program and I don't have a choice of what science to choose because they only offer Chemistry at HL!" Unfortunately, that is just a fact of life. Not a single school will offer *all* the IB subject choices that are available, so you need to make the best out of the situation. Don't waste your time protesting and making petitions asking your school to introduce a subject that would probably yield high demand from the students. It's much more complicated than that as there are monetary, time and faculty constraints that need to be taken into account.

In certain specific circumstances however, there are ways in which you can 'create' a new subject for yourself. You could potentially sit the two years in a HL class only to then undertake the SL exam. This may be frowned upon by your school, but try to see if this is possible.

I initially started the IB program with the intention of doing four HL subjects (Economics, Mathematics, Geography and Physics) as opposed to the usual three. However, as the time came to make final exam choices, I realised that I would be better off dropping one of my HLs rather than risking getting a lower grade. Physics HL was unfortunately a bit too demanding for me, and I argued that it took away too much revision time from my other HL subjects in which I was trying to achieve 7s. So I repeatedly asked the IB coordinator to be allowed to sit the SL Physics exam, and continue to sit the Physics HL class. Eventually all the details were sorted out and it worked out fine.

Another good friend of mine knew from the start that he wanted to sit the SL English exam, however he realised that if he attended the HL English class he would be better prepared due to the more challenging nature of the HL course. I'm not saying sit HL classes for all of your subjects, but this is certainly an overlooked tactic for the more ambitious students out there. If you are not challenged enough and would find it beneficial learning some HL material despite sitting the SL class then try to make that possible by carefully discussing it with your IB coordinator. Note also that the HL teacher may be much 'better' than the SL one.

At the end of the day the choice of which subjects you will do will largely depend on how the schedule blocks in your school work and what subjects they actually have on offer. Don't make a huge fuss if you can't get exactly what you want. There are thousands of students out there in similar situations – if not worse. Work with what you have. Take my tips listed above, consult your parents, consult your teachers, consult your older school friends and hopefully this will help you reach a decision.

Do not choose a subject "because my friend is doing it as well." This is probably the dumbest thing you can do when it comes to making subject choices. Chances are you and your "friends" will see each other in other classes, and you'll have enough time to hang out outside of class. So please, do yourself a favour and don't follow your favourite peers around like a tail.

Stuck with non-ideal IB subject choices? Not to worry. Just flip to the relevant chapters in this book and I'll show you how to pass with flying colours no matter what subjects you choose to do.

A DAY IN THE LIFE OF IB

The purpose of this chapter is to provide some basic guidelines you should follow in order to survive in the world of IB. The degree to which you follow the advice in this chapter really depends on what type of student you are. If organization, motivation and promptness are second nature to you then you will find most of the information in this chapter somewhat obvious.

Attendance

Although some of your classmates may beg to differ, missing school does not make you a modern day Ferris Bueller. You must ensure that you are attending class as often as you can. Most of your classes are very demanding, and even one or two days missed could mean a lot in terms of catching up with the material. No matter how useless you think a certain class is, I would still recommend you show up because it is good work ethic and it will keep you busy. Exceptions can be made as you edge closer to exams. I have known some students to miss almost 2 days per week during the final month of IB because they felt that home revision was more productive.

In the rare case that you miss class because of an illness or any other valid reason, make sure that you talk to your teacher and get the correct material that you may have missed. Those of you who skip class regularly will find that sympathy is hard to come by when you have a genuine reason for your tardiness. This is yet another reason to avoid unnecessarily skipping class.

Free Periods

The term 'free period' has varying interpretations from student to student and school to school. To some of you this may mean an hour of playing solitaire on your laptop, to others it may mean an opportunity to finish last night's homework. Similarly, some schools are more stringent than others. At my school most teachers treated 'free periods' as a quiet one-hour study session where students were free to do work independently. I want you to make the most out of the time available. Whether you do work, socialize, or catch up on sleep – make sure that it is not time wasted and that you are doing something that will benefit your grades in the long run.

Some schools allow students to arrive later (if the free periods are in the morning) or to depart before school is over (if the free periods are in the afternoon). Find out if you can do the same, and decide whether you would benefit from this. On occasion I would try to miss any free period at the end of the day and get home to catch up on some sleep. You need to work out whether this is possible, and feasible.

Understandably, some schools simply do not allow students to have 'free periods'. Many of you studying in the US will find that any period not devoted to the IB will be packed with an alternative high school curriculum. Some schools prefer to devote more time to extra-curricular activities, or keep students busy with extra classes. If this is the case, then great. As long as you are being kept busy and productive, then you are on the right track.

Note Taking

Personally, I was never that great at taking notes in class. My handwriting was poor, and I found it difficult to take in everything that was being discussed and simultaneously jot down effective notes. I figured that if I can engage in the conversation and understand what the teacher is trying to say, then I could write down more effective notes after class. Unfortunately, too often I would forget.

Effective note taking is not something that can be learned in a few months, let alone a few weeks. It took me nearly two years of university lectures to finally be able to write and process information fast enough to take very helpful notes.

I find that this habit differs in difficulty across students. If handwriting is your biggest concern, try to bring a laptop. A more drastic alternative (and one that should only really be used during the most important and difficult sessions) would be to bring a voice recorder and make notes afterwards. Of course this involves a great deal of dedication and motivation; however I do remember certain HL Mathematics classes where a voice recorder proved to be a life-saver.

There are two key things to remember when taking notes. One is to make sure that everything you write down isn't already explained in detail in your textbook and/or previous notes. This is very inefficient and you are better off simply listening and letting the information sink into your memory. The second thing to keep in mind is to only write down notes that make sense. If you find yourself writing words that are unfamiliar to you, then you are wasting your time. You need to raise your hand and ask the question.

You may find yourself lucky enough to have a friend or two who take outstanding notes. Although getting great notes from a fellow peer is better than having nothing at all, I would still be cautious before resorting to this option. No matter how good the notes are, they will never be as valuable to you as something you wrote down yourself.

Organisation

If I had an IB point for every time I heard someone mutter the words, 'What? We had homework?' I would have a lot of points. Keeping an agenda or a daily planner is a very simple solution to keeping track of what is due when. Make a habit of writing down important dates as soon as you hear about them. The IB does a pretty good job at reminding students about the big deadlines (Extended Essay, External Assessment, CAS portfolio) however any internal deadlines you may have are your responsibility to note.

There's no reason to go old-school when it comes to organisation. With the rise in popularity of iPhones, Blackberry's, and personal laptops, it has become much easier for you to electronically set reminders. These items are also more likely to be consulted, and less likely to be lost than a simple paperback agenda. You could also double up a paperback agenda with a Google Calendar or something else that is available online.

Health

As I mentioned before, this is NOT a self-help book, nor do I ever intend to offer life advice to anyone. However, I do think it is worthwhile at least briefly mentioning the importance of things like eating right and exercising well.

Research has shown time and time again that physical activity is crucial in maintaining mental well-being. IB students often report negative moods, irritability, and other stress-related problems. All of this can lead to more complicated emotional concerns. Exercise is a good combatant in your fight to a healthy physical and mental well-being.

Even just 20 minutes of exercise can lead to higher energy levels. You will find it easier to sit down and concentrate on your studies and may even feel more motivated. Also, you can easily combine exercise with socialising. Having someone to talk to while jogging or at the gym can be a great stress-reliever – just make sure the conversation steers clear of IB-related matters.

Just as important as regular exercise is keeping an eye on what you are eating. If you ever felt exhausted despite not really doing anything, or get easily distracted when you should be working, this could be down to your choice or lack of foods.

Although our brain is only about 2% of our total body mass, it consumes roughly 20% of the energy you take in. When we concentrate the brain uses up to 200 kilocalories per hour – or 10% of your daily food intake. So next time you skip breakfast, or have a very late lunch keep in mind that your brain needs a steady supply of nutrients – many of which come from food.

Homework

When it comes to doing homework it is very difficult to prescribe specific advice because people have different preferences that work best for them. Personally, I found that doing homework in the late evening or at night was the most effective. This worked for me as there were little distractions and there was a sense of urgency which kept me motivated.

Besides timing, you also need to consider working effectively for concentrated amounts of time with no breaks. Ideally, working for 20 minutes non-stop with no outside interference and then rewarding yourself with a small break seems to be among the ideal strategies. Some of you may find that you work best with music in the background, or that your multitasking skills are so good that you can afford to flip your computer tabs from Facebook to iTunes to your Lab Report every few minutes. It's difficult to change this habit, and unless it is seriously damaging the quality of your work, I would not worry too much about it.

One tip that I found to work very nicely when doing homework was to save my favourite material for last. Getting all the difficult and less-enjoyable work out of the way early will not only lessen the chances of simply not doing it, but you will also have something to look forward to. Of course, one should be careful not to rush through the harder material just for the sake of 'getting it out of the way' before moving on to the more enjoyable material.

Be heard

No matter how timid and shy you may be, there will be days when you simply need to make a formal comment or complaint about something that concerns you. In order to do this you need to build a constructive relationship with your IB Coordinator and any other influential teachers. This is much easier said than done.

Learn how to talk to authoritative figures. If you book a meeting with your IB Coordinator, then do not show up unprepared. If you show them that you care, they will care too. The same goes for most teachers. If you show an interest and a longing for help (perhaps by asking for a contact email to reach them at after-school hours) then they are more than likely to respond positively.

INTERNAL ASSESSMENT

Internal Assessment (IA) is the easiest, most effective and fastest way to get top marks in almost all of your subjects. You would have to be extremely ignorant and/or stupid to ignore that fact. Try doing some simple math. If we say that, on average, IA takes up roughly 25% of your grade for each subject then that means it takes up ¼ of the maximum grade 7 per subject – nearly two entire points. Now, this may not seem like much, but when you consider that you have 6 subjects plus the 3 bonus points from TOK/EE – this adds up to 15 points towards your IB diploma. Simply put: from maxing out on your Internal Assessment and EE/TOK you can get 15 points even before you step into the examination room.

That is the beauty of it. You have no idea what a comforting feeling it is walking into the exam room knowing you already have 12 – 15 points in the bag. One must try to remain realistic. No matter how much you have studied, no matter how many past papers you have done, and no matter how well you have grasped the material, what happens on the exam day will to a certain extent be outside of your control. What if you break an arm, get a stomach ache or become ill during the exam? What if all three happen? What if your co-coordinator makes a mistake and forgets to give you a periodic table for your HL Chemistry exam (as has happened)? What if you just "go blank" when you open your exam and forget all that you have crammed the night before?

I have seen some of the best IB candidates underperform on exam day simply because of bad luck and misfortune. Another likely scenario is that you are simply not an exam person. I myself am usually very comfortable with the material, spend plenty of time studying, and usually am able to answer most questions when asked verbally in a non-exam situation. However, when the clock is ticking and the pressure is on, I tend to only perform at about 80% of my potential. I am not an "exam person". In fact I hate examinations because so many factors are outside of your control. There are too many ways in which one can make careless mistakes and mess up.

As I was trying to point out, IA makes up roughly 25% of your grade for each subject. In subjects such as English it amounts to nearly 50% of the grade. So even before you sit your English exam, you are nearly 50% done. This means that if you have done amazingly well on your IA, you already have 3 or 4 marks secured towards your English grade. It is a very comforting feeling to know that no matter how poorly you perform on your exam, you are almost definitely in the 4 to 7 range – in other words you are comfortably going to pass. This may not mean much to the more ambitious candidates reading this manual. If you are amongst the IB candidates who worry about failing the IB diploma then this IA stuff can save you.

At the moment, some of you may still need further convincing that Internal Assessment is extremely important. The words 'lab report', 'economic commentary' and 'World Literature paper' are so often used in the same breath as the word 'homework' that students forget to realise the importance of IA. The points add up, and before you know it, it might be too late to go back and capitalize on your IA marks.

Let's think about this logically. The assessment is usually given a week or even a few weeks in advance. For bigger assignments such as the World Literature paper or a HL Mathematics Portfolio you have substantially more time to prepare. You are given weeks to complete something that will account for a generous fraction of your final grade. Now contrast this with the final examinations, which will usually take up the remaining 60% - 75% of the final grade. The exam duration per subject is rarely more than 6 or 7 hours. Those few hours will decide what you will get for the remaining portion of your grade. Would it not make sense then to work relentlessly on maximizing your mark for the IA simply because you are given so much more time and space? The final examination goes by in the blink of an eye whereas you are given an abundance of time to work on your IA. Are you starting to see what I mean?

You are given weeks, if not months, to decide nearly a third of your grade, and then you are given two or three hours to decide the remaining two-thirds. It would be foolish to put in less effort for the IA then the actual examinations. They are practically handing you these marks. No matter how poorly you know the material, or how poorly you perform on examinations, nearly anyone can ace their Internal Assessment – especially given the advice provided further in this guide.

So if you are one of those people who tend to underperform in examinations and simply can't be bothered to study, you absolutely need to take full advantage of the IA. It baffles me as to why so many students fail to see this loophole. Even the top IB candidates often focus so much on learning the material and doing well in the actual exams that they lose track of the fact that IA also counts towards the final grade.

With regards to the order of importance for IB-related daily matter, I would suggest the following rank: 1) Internal Assessment, 2) revision for tests, 3) homework. This means that if you have a lab report due in tomorrow and a test as well, you need to finish and polish the lab before you even start thinking about revising for the test. Tests will come and go, but you will have few opportunities to redo your Internal Assessments.

All the labs, coursework, portfolios and papers that are sent off as part of your IA are of far greater importance than any test or homework assignment that you have to do. Yes, your trimester grade may suffer. Yes, the teacher may get on your back for not doing the homework. Nonetheless, you need to keep a voice in the back of your head telling you that "at the end of the day, small tests and homework won't give me my 7s, the IB Internal Assessment will."

The beauty behind Internal Assessment is that literally anyone, of any academic ability, can get top marks. This is great news for those of you who do not plan on studying much for the exams, or who are terrified of test-taking. All you need to do is spend an incredible amount of time constantly improving and upgrading your assignment. I have seen some pretty daft IB students ace their assignments simply because they spent day and night perfecting them. Although they may have not been academically gifted, at least they realised the potential impact that IA could have on their grades – and in that sense they are geniuses.

It doesn't matter whether you are "smart" or "dumb". You simply need to be ruthless when it comes to completing your assignments. Follow the guidelines that I provide in this book for each subject on how to maximize your IA. If you do that, then regardless of how good or bad you *think* you are at a certain subject, you will be able to get a "handicap" of +2 on your final grade before you sit the exam.

You need to become the King (or Queen) of IA in your class. All the other students will be in awe as you get 19/20 back for your portfolio or an "excellent" for your Economics commentary. They may say you are wasting your time aiming for the perfect IA assessment, but when you get your final grades back you will be laughing at them. You need to strive to have the best coursework possible.

I remember a few months before final examinations some teachers would announce whose work was getting sent off to be moderated. Now, I don't know how the system works inside out, but I have an instinctive feeling that for most Internal Assessment the IBO demands that a good distribution of student work is sent off. In other words: the top assignments, the average assignments and the assignments at the lower end of the grading scale. I would look around the class to see who else was having their work sent off, and immediately I could tell that my work was part of the "top assignments". This took a lot of stress off the final examinations. It is an incredible feeling when you are revising to know that you are 25% closer to getting your 7s.

Getting top marks in your IA is not an easy task. Then again, neither is getting 7s in your examinations. The key difference is that whereas with the exams you are given a few hours to show your worth, the IA timeline is much more generous. You will need to work late nights, weekends, and holidays in order to get top marks for your IA. In fact, you would probably work just as hard (if not harder) a few weeks prior to your exams, so I don't see why this would be such a daunting task.

You need to develop a habit of wanting to strive for perfection in all of your externally moderated assignments. Treat this as being just as important as the actual exam, or even more so. I want you to start feeling extremely disappointed if you are getting back labs/commentaries/portfolios that are below a grade 6. Not only should you be getting 7s, you should be getting high 7s. Keep in mind that what your teacher thinks you deserve is not the final grade. It will be moderated and probably hiked up or down a few notches. You should therefore make sure to leave a little room for change when you are told your predicted IB grades.

You may struggle getting 6s or even 5s on your school tests. At the same time, you may be a student who is borderline failing the diploma program and is anticipating the worst when the final examinations come around. In either case, this advice about IA is of equal importance. IA can turn a failing IB diploma grade of 15 to a 30. Or a 30 to a 45. The important thing is that you take this advice and follow it through.

I firmly believe that if a student maxes out on his/her IA, then it is nearly impossible to fail the IB diploma. You will get somewhere around 15 marks for your assignments alone (given that you get all 3 bonus marks), which leaves just about 10 more marks from your actual examination. I have yet to meet a person that cannot scrape 10 marks on their actual examinations. If you maximize your IA marks, then you are entering a stress-free world of examinations. Instead of deciding where you will be on a scale of zero to 45, you now can estimate your final grade on a scale of 15 to 45.

I know I am getting repetitive but you need to drill this into your head. You need to strive for perfection on your Internal Assessment Do that and you are one step, one giant leap, closer to getting what you want from your IB diploma. Don't be ignorant, realise the power of IA marks and the effect that they can have on your final grade. You don't know how much you will hate yourself when you find out that the reason you missed out on getting your dream grade of 45 was due to a poorly done World Literature paper that dragged you down to a 44 overall. Or how about finding out that the only reason you failed IB was because you "forgot" to hand in an Economics commentary and this dragged you down below 24 marks. Be smart: milk the IA for all that it is worth.

It's a miracle that a notoriously "rigorous" program such as the IB diploma program would have nearly 25% of the final score decided on a non-exam basis. You are lucky that final grades aren't based entirely on your ability to perform well in exams as is the case in many other high school programs worldwide. This provides a great opportunity to those of you who are hard working and intelligent, yet lack that cutting edge when it comes to examinations. Take full advantage of this – it won't be long before the IB starts to diminish the importance of Internal Assessment and adds greater value to the actual examinations.

CAS

This chapter will be kept very short. If you are honestly struggling to get the hours that you need for CAS then I cannot do much for you except shake my head in disappointment. The good thing about CAS is that it gets everyone involved in the community, teaches students to be creative and aims to keep everyone in good health. The sad thing is: if you were really that concerned with community service, wouldn't you be doing it already, instead of being "rewarded" for it with CAS hours? However, that is not our concern. Your aim is to get your hours and finish CAS as soon as you can (preferably the middle of your first IB year) with minimal difficulty.

As part of your "core" IB requirements (which include the EE and TOK components) you are obliged to complete the CAS program. This means that you must achieve a set minimum amount of hours in each of the three components: Creativity, Action and Service.

Creativity
Probably the 2nd easiest CAS component to fulfil; you don't need to be a young Mozart or Picasso to get your creativity hours. First and foremost,

engage in the school's creativity activities. This includes any play productions, choirs, and art competitions. If that doesn't work out for you, do something independent for the school community. Design their website, make a new banner/poster to boost school spirit, teach younger students how to draw/Photoshop/act. It's pretty easy to get your hours for Creativity, just don't leave it too late.

Action

This should be very straightforward. I know what it's like to be lazy and non-athletic more than anyone else, but even I managed to get my hours with absolute ease. I joined the school sports teams not only for the sportive factor but also simply because it was a lot of fun. If you go through high-school never having tried out for the football, basketball, swimming, volleyball, tennis or even track and field teams then you are missing out on a lot of memorable experiences.

You can't honestly say that there is a struggle to find activities to fulfil your "Action" hours requirement. Even the non-athletic kids at my school somehow found their way to the local gym and at least lifted some weights or did some treadmill running. There is always some solution available.

Service

This is the problem area for most people. I don't think it's because we are all inherently selfish and egotistical, but it is perhaps more to do with a problem in finding service work. If your CAS coordinator (assuming your school *has* a CAS coordinator) is living up to the expectations then you should be able to get advice and opportunities via him/her. I know schools treat CAS and especially the service component in varying degrees of seriousness. Nonetheless, you need to ensure you did enough to make the IB moderator satisfied if your portfolio is sent off.

The type of service you do will largely depend on where you live, how comfortable you are being outdoors, how fluent you are in the domestic language, and a variety of other factors that would make it too difficult to give you any specific tasks. Like I said before, no one is asking you to create a charity overnight or clean oil spills and create peace in the Middle East. You just need to demonstrate that you care enough about the community and do the hours required.

Some examples of service work done at my previous school included: charities, hospital work, building work, working at a retirement home, and free tutoring for specific skills.

CAS Coordinator

As mentioned, the school's CAS coordinator will largely decide the success of your CAS program. When I did the IB, the CAS coordinator was wonderful. Not only did he make sure that everyone did what was required of them, he also made sure that those who tried to cheat the system were sufficiently punished. Your CAS coordinator will either be very engaging and hunt you down if you are lacking on the hours (for your own good of course) or he will be easy-going and let you decide what you want to do and when you want to do it. The latter approach is a bit too risky for my liking.

At the end of the day you just have to make the best of what you've got. If your CAS coordinator doesn't seem to care about whether you pass or not, then that just means you will have to work that little bit extra than the student who has a CAS coordinator who does everything for him. Having a poorly run CAS program is not a good enough reason for failing to meet the CAS component requirements.

Tips

Although my CAS advice lacks much detail, I can offer you a few words of advice on the CAS program in general.

<u>Completion</u> – make sure you complete the CAS program as early as possible. I'm not saying you give up on all creative, athletic and community related aspects of your life for the remainder of your IB experience; however, it will be more beneficial for you to complete CAS as soon as possible. I was done with most of the CAS requirements before I stepped into 12th grade. This did require a lot of work to be done while I was in 11th grade (including many weekends working, and also a school trip to help build/paint a school in Morocco during Fall break).

My IB coordinator offered the opportunity to begin CAS work as early as 10th grade (a year before IB began). Those who seized this opportunity were rewarded because they would have the entire last year of their IB without the CAS burden on their shoulders. I had friends who were being chased down for a good part of grade 12 and this stress reflected on their other IB work. The lesson here is that the sooner you finish CAS, the sooner you can start to worry about all the other work you have to juggle for the IB. Get this out of the way as soon as you can – even if that means working in hospitals and running marathons every weekend in your first few months of IB.

<u>Writing the Portfolio</u> – make sure you keep a very clean and tidy track of all your CAS activities. For some activities that exceed a certain amount of hours, you will be required to write up an evaluation. Do this as soon as you finish the work, otherwise you will just forget what you did. Keep all this information in a very safe place and don't lose it because there will come a day when your CAS coordinator will ask for it.

<u>Faking It</u> – just don't do it. How hard is it to legitimately do the hours? If you think you can forge your tennis coach's signature, then don't act too surprised when your CAS coordinator calls him up only to find out you never did the 10 hours of tennis lessons that you claimed. There's nothing more sneaky and deceitful than claiming you helped your community when really all you did was just cheat. You will probably get caught and feel guilty as you are made an example of in front of your friends. Just do the hours – it's really not that much to ask.

While on the subject of misconduct, please avoid asking for CAS hours when you know you didn't deserve them. This includes doing paid work, tasks for your family, favours for your friends, and any other clever ideas you might have to score some easy CAS hours. Examples include kids who lie about jogging at home and forge their parents' signatures, or those who claim to do unpaid work for their parent's company. Don't end up like this. Not only do you risk being caught, you're also better off just doing the hours and benefiting from the experience.

University

One massive advantage that you will have over other non-IB university applicants (and even job applicants) is that you can use your CAS experience to build up your CV/application. Community service looks great when applying to competitive universities, as do creative abilities and an athletic lifestyle. Make the most use of your CAS program at school because it will be of great use in later life. Even in my current CV I still have elements of community service that I did during CAS.

For this very reason, I strongly suggest that you make full use of your CAS program and do service activities that are more attractive than others. For example, organizing a concert at the retirement home is a lot more eye-catching on your CV than handing out pamphlets or walking dogs. In fact any service work that requires engagement with people you would not normally work with is very impressive to universities and employers. For this reason you should ensure to do CAS service activities that actually mean something. Similarly, playing for the school football team is more effective than spending an hour a day at the gym because it shows that you can cooperate with others and work in a team. Choose activities that you might want to impress with later on in life.

Failure

If you fail your entire IB Diploma because you did not meet the CAS requirements then there is little hope for you. I have seen some of the worst IB candidates still manage to scrape through their CAS hours so for you this definitely should not be a problem. Don't overestimate CAS as it really should not dominate your IB schedule. Then again, don't leave it last on your to-do list because it will harm your other IB work.

REVISION

Preparing for the final exams can be a daunting task. Once the examination timetable is published your first exam date will remain cemented in your mind. Although there are hundreds, if not thousands, of ways to revise for the examinations, many are largely ineffective and far too time consuming. In this chapter I will give you some general guidelines for how to best revise for your final exams.

Time Management

Having me preach to you about the importance of time management is perhaps hypocrisy at its best. For me it was not until I got into university that I really started to understand how effective time management can be. If you are one of the lucky few who have mastered the skill at an early age then consider yourself lucky. This is an invaluable ability that you will use regularly throughout your life.

One of the great rewards of undertaking the IB challenge is that you will have the opportunity to learn amazing time-management skills. The key to good time management is not just writing up a good schedule, but also imposing consequences when you fail to adhere to that schedule. For example if you promised to revise biology for 45 minutes a day every weekday, and then you only manage to do 15 minutes on one of days you must make sure you catch up on the remaining half an hour the day after.

When Do I Start?

I had a teacher who once told the class (with 4 months remaining until final exams), "I hope your revision is going well... and if there are still some of you that haven't started revising, well you are already behind." Hearing those words I got uncomfortably nervous and stressed. Not only had I not begun revising, I didn't even know where to start. Several weeks passed as I procrastinated even more and eventually "mock exams" came around. I didn't study much, except for glancing over a few past papers from the previous year. Luckily, it turned out that some of the "mock exams" were in fact last year's actual examinations. Nonetheless, I didn't have a good feeling about the whole thing and my grades reflected this – got a 36 overall with a 4 in HL Mathematics. This was a real wake up call as my university offer was given on the condition that I get a minimum of 40 points overall and a 7 in HL Mathematics and Economics. I feared the worst.

With less than a month to revise and no quick solution in sight, I was probably justified in my distress. Some of my friends had been "revising" since the beginning of winter break. I was too busy partying and procrastinating. With less than a month to go for exams I knew that this month would make or break me. I quickly made a demanding exam schedule and started it the following day. For a whole month I practically lived in a cave, having deactivated Facebook and deleted Skype. I read, breathed and lived revision. The only thing that kept me going was a voice in the back of my head telling me "you did nothing for two years, the least you can do is work mercilessly for one month, and then it will be all over."

The whole point of that little story is not to suggest that you should only leave a month for revision. It was simply to demonstrate to you what you will have to go through if you do leave revision so late. I was never one to miss a party – there was no way I could give up weekends, and sports, and all my hobbies just so that I could start revision many months in advance. I left revision too late, but, I paid the price. Whatever choice you make, you need to realise that you will have to bear the consequences when your actual exam preparation comes around.

There is no *ideal* time to start revising. That being said, you should never leave less than a month, and you would probably be wasting your time starting revision any sooner than 3 months before exams. Some of you may seem confused as to why I am suggesting that you don't study *too much*, but that's not what I am saying. There have been studies done that show how students can reach the "peak" of their revision too early, and have a "meltdown" before actual exams. This usually happens to students that start revising nearly a year in advance. By revising too much in advance you may run the risk of failing to recall the earliest information and start to panic.

Perhaps the golden rule to IB exam revision can be worked out logically. If you still have assignments to finish that will be graded by the IB, it's probably safe to say that you should not even think about starting revising. Your Internal Assessment is far more important than early revision so make sure you get that out the way first. Once all your work has been sent off you can drop everything else and just focus on revising for your exams. Always remember your priorities: first get all the IA out of the way, and then you can concentrate all your attention on revision.

The IB is too demanding for you to be starting revision early. With all the tests, assignments, sports meetings, CAS reports and homework that you will have on your hands, you will not be able to begin preparing too much in advance. Don't forget however that all the tests and coursework that you are doing *is* a form a revision. It's not the best, but at least you are doing something to reinforce your knowledge of the subject. So don't think you are doomed if you haven't been revising out of a textbook with a month to go before exams. You have been revising "indirectly". At least that's what I told myself in order to be able to sleep at night.

Mock Examinations

Most schools will administer "mock" examinations several weeks or months prior to the actual exams. If not, I strongly suggest you ask the school to set them up. This is not really a test of your knowledge and how well you will perform on the actual exam. It's more to get you familiar with examination conduct and protocol. You will need to get used to arriving punctually, having the right materials, and following the exam rules and regulations.

Nonetheless, I suggest you make full use of your mock exams and treat them almost as if they were the real deal. You will be able to see what you would achieve if you had sat the real exam and not done any revision. Thus it is kind of a test of how focused you were in class throughout the year. For most of you this experience will be a wake-up call.

Once your mock exam results come out don't just glance at the grade and move forward. Find out where you went wrong and where you could have done better. Although these exams are graded by your teachers, it doesn't mean the marking will be much different when done by examiners elsewhere. Look for places where you lost marks due to silly mistakes and try to work on these mistakes before your real examination.

One final note on mock examinations. It is no hidden secret that most schools use last year's real paper as the current year's mock paper. Don't think that you are a genius for figuring this out. This has been a tradition in most schools; however some now started to come up with new material. Nonetheless, if your mock exam paper happens to be a past paper that you have already worked on yourself then don't feel guilty or feel like you didn't deserve the grade you got. If you did well that just shows that your work with past papers has been worthwhile. You were able to apply the material again, meaning you probably learnt something along the way. If you still did poorly despite having seen the paper and the markscheme beforehand then you have reason to worry.

What do I revise?

You should by now realise that you will not be devoting an equal share of revision time to each subject. Some subjects you may not even bother with until perhaps a week before the final exam. Other subjects you may like to start revising several months in advance. This will all depend on what your strengths are, as well as what your aims are.

For example; my IB results needed to coincide with my university offer from Oxford – I didn't really care about much else. This meant that I needed a 40 overall, 7s in HL Mathematics and HL Economics, as well as 6s in all of my remaining subjects. As soon as I learnt of this offer, I immediately outlined my problem areas. I knew that getting a 7 in HL Mathematics was by far my greatest weakness. I had never gotten a 7 in any test, and was probably averaging out a 5 overall. I felt uncomfortable with a large portion of the material. I also knew that getting a minimum of 6 in HL Geography and SL English should not be too big of a problem. I felt very comfortable with the Geography material, and my IA for English seemed good enough. Having gone over all of this in my head, I began to formulate how I will go about revising. I ended up spending more than 50% of my revision on Mathematics (doing a past paper almost every other night), then 30% on Economics (because I couldn't take any risks as I had to get a 7) and the rest of time I divided equally amongst the remaining subjects.

This may come as a shock to a lot of you. How can one spend more than half of their revision time on just one subject? Instinctively you would want to divide your time equally amongst the six subjects giving you an equal chance of doing well in all of them. This is not the correct way to think. You need to identify your weaknesses and base your revision around this. If you are borderline failing Chemistry and sailing through Business Management, then focus all your attention on getting through the Chemistry material. You may not enjoy it as much as BM but it's by far more important to you and your overall grade.

Figure out what your problem areas are by looking at your predicted grades and talking to your teachers to check where you stand in terms of their predictions. More importantly, you should know by now what your aims and objectives are. Do you need a minimum of a 6 in this subject for university or university credits? Do you need to get a 7 in this in order to fulfil the requirements? Once you work out what you are aiming for then make sure to focus your energy on this specifically. If you don't have any set aims and you are just trying to get the greatest points total then your task may be slightly easier.

How Do I Revise?

Although there are a multitude of methods to revise for the actual exams, you need to be careful and avoid doing redundant tasks. Out of all the possible methods that are out there, I highly recommend you try to focus your revision around past papers. For a full detailed explanation of this method please refer to the specified chapter on Past Papers.

I know that this method may not work for everyone. Perhaps you made great notes throughout the year or you enjoy learning from the syllabus and the textbook. Nonetheless, more often than not the most successful IB candidates will tell you that they revised primarily with the help of past papers and markschemes.

If you still insist on studying from textbooks and notes, I recommend you cover some basic study tips. For example, some subjects such as biology may require more 'visual learner' skills – using your eyes and memory to recall the information. I know some students get very creative with this process and create highly effective 'mind maps' and 'word association' memory tools. I guess the theme here is sticking to the revision method that you know works for *you* the best. If you don't think you have one, I highly suggest you get cracking on past papers.

No matter what method you choose, I highly recommend that your revision remains active. By this I mean you are constantly writing, making notes, and writing again. Although lying in the grass with a book to cover your face from the sun sounds like a good plan, you are wasting your time. Sit at a desk, grab some plain white paper, and make good use of your pen and pencil. You are twice as likely to remember what you are revising if you are constantly writing and not just glancing over material.

Some of you may find that study groups work well for particular subjects. I myself found it extremely useful to work together on a maths paper with another person, or to discuss economics material in a group. Choose your groups wisely though. Avoid students who are far more advanced than you and avoid friends that seem like they attend revision sessions more for the social aspect rather than actual studying. The point is that if you find revising or working through past papers with a group of equally motivated peers useful then by all means proceed with that.

You will probably have a good week or two of no school before your examinations begin so make full use of that period. Make sure each day is productive and that you set yourself mental tasks to complete every day. Don't be alarmed but you should probably be aiming to get at least 7 hours of pure revision done every day that week. This isn't really asking that much given that you probably haven't been doing much revision all year.

Don't panic if you come across something during your revision that you have never seen before. Chances are it probably isn't in the syllabus anymore or maybe you just missed it out in class. Ask your friends or your teacher for advice. You shouldn't spend hours and hours stuck on one section or problem of new material – remember this should be revision and not first-time learning.

Another common mistake made during the revision period is setting yourself goals that are simply beyond your reach. No one expects you to revise for twelve hours a day straight, sleep for eight and leave four hours for washing/pooping/eating. It shouldn't have to come to that. You should be studying hard but also leaving a little time to relax and recover.

Remember that there is a huge amount of resources available for you to aid in your revision, all of which I discuss in more depth in the Resources chapter.

Cramming: The Night Before

No words of advice or comfort can really help ease your pre-exam stress and make you relax the night before your first examination. You will remember that date for a long time. For most of you, this is probably the first official externally graded examination that you take (unless you've done GCSEs or SATs). This can be a scary notion but you just need to realise that in a matter of a few weeks all of this will be over and you will embark on the longest holiday of your teenage life.

Now, what should you be doing the night before an exam? Well, as a golden rule, you should restrict your revising only on material for which you will be examined the *following day*. This means if you have a math exam tomorrow, you should be doing just math today – not biology which you have in a weeks' time or something like that. You need to keep the subject fresh and familiar in your mind – focus all your energy on it the night before and hopefully you will wake up with most of it still in your head.

Now, what about cramming? There is a heated debate as to whether cramming even works. Some say that having late night cram sessions is not only ineffective, but that it can put you in unnecessary stress and increase your chances of "going blank" the following day. Others will tell you that cramming is the best form of revision, and everything you stuff into your brain the night before just spills on your exam paper the next morning. Then there are also those who will tell you that cramming works – but you should not do it because you are not learning long-term, you are merely memorizing stuff in the short-term which you will probably forget in a weeks' time. Those people are missing the point.

From a personal viewpoint, cramming the night before an IB examination was helpful, but only to a certain extent (and only for certain subjects). For example I found that cramming popular mathematic proofs was extremely helpful, however cramming an English novel was not. Use your common sense a little. More importantly, don't overdo it. Your sleep and nutrition can play a large role in your examinations, so make sure you're getting a minimum of 6 hours of sleep most of the days. Exceptions can be made when you have an exam the following day, and then after that you have a day or two break from exams for recovery – in that scenario I have seen some students even pull off near all-nighters.

Cramming in the mornings, just hours prior to the exam, is another viable option for those of you who like to get to bed early. Also, it goes almost without saying that for exams where you need to memorise extensive formulae, jot down the most important ones that you crammed as soon as the exam begins.

Disappointment: The Morning After

However well your exam went you are more than likely to come out feeling rather disappointed. This is natural. If you come out of the exam room very cheery and happy that usually means that either you have been very lucky and really aced it, or you really messed up a question or two because you misunderstood what was being asked. Either way, the most important thing to remember after every examination is to move on. Don't hang around outside the exam halls asking all your friends what they answered or what they thought of a certain question. The exam is over. Whatever you say or do after is not going to change what you wrote on that paper or the outcome of the exam. You need to revise for your other papers.

This is the one of the biggest mistakes I see students make when it comes to revision. Instead of studying for the next paper, they waste time talking to their friends and trying to figure out how they got this or that answer, or what they wrote about in their essay. You are likely to get even more disappointed and discouraged if you waste time asking your friends what they wrote down only to find out that your answer was totally different. After you have just sat an examination, just go home as fast as you can and focus on the next one.

Moreover, if you have finished the last paper for a certain subject, then make sure you get that subject totally out of your head. Clear all the notes and papers for that subject out of the way and pretend that you don't even know what it is. Instead of doing 6 subjects, you are now only doing 5. It is of vital importance that you make the transition from one subject to the next as smooth as you can as the exam schedules can be very hectic.

Method of Elimination: A Technique

One factor that separates the more successful exam candidates from the others is that they have picked up certain examination techniques along the way. One of these is a revision technique by which you use process of elimination to make an educated guess as to what might show up on the next paper. Let me give you an example: when I sat my HL Economics exam, Paper 1 had a big question on monopolies, but neither Paper 1 nor 2 had anything on negative externalities. I made an educated guess that there would be a big question on negative externalities on the Paper 3, with little emphasis on monopolies. This was indeed the case that year.

You can do this for almost any paper. Each subject has its key syllabus areas on which students should be examined. This is perhaps more true for Group 3, 4 and 5 subjects than the others. You can use a process of elimination to make a clever guess as to what could potentially show up on the next paper having already sat the first one. Discuss this with your friends as they probably have a similar inkling. This technique, combined with cramming, can practically make you an overnight expert on an area with which you were previously not that comfortable.

Last Minute Revision

You need to make full use of the last few moments before you enter the examination room. Find a nice quiet place to quickly run through key points and get any last minute cramming done. Avoid large groups of people as you will probably not be able to concentrate that well. You should probably even revise in the car/bus ride to the examination place. Just don't waste any valuable time that you have on useless distractions.

STRESS MANAGEMENT

There is no hiding from the fact that the IB Diploma programme can be very stressful. There will be certain weeks or days where you will feel like you are juggling 6 plates with the weight of the academic world on your shoulders and a ball and chain with the words 'EE and TOK' around your legs. Nonetheless, I will now introduce a few tips to help you deal with the strain and anxiety.

Nutrition:

The stereotype of the IB student as someone surviving on caffeine, Pot Noodles, and energy drinks is, in many cases, not a complete exaggeration. If you are up late at night busy working then you are more likely to consume foods and drinks that require little time to prepare and give a good energy boost.

Although I have already reminded you about the benefits of eating right during your two years in the IB program, the exam period itself will pose its own challenges. Even if you are franticly revising all day and all night, try to still get your three meals a day and eat plenty of vitamin rich foods.

I found myself chewing a lot of gum during late nights and revision stages. Personally, I found that this helped me focus more and kept me awake. Those of you that smoke will probably find that you are smoking a lot more than normal. If you are a big coffee fan, then be careful not to overdo it.

Sleep

I'll be first to admit that the amount of sleep you will get during the two year IB program will probably be less than any other two year period of your life. On any given day, I could spot several of my fellow students drifting off during class, or having serious bags under their eyes from a lack of sleep.

Making sure that you get enough sleep is once again due to good time management skills. I found that I would come home from school too tired to be productive so I would make it a habit to get a couple hours of sleep in the evening. Usually this would just be on the couch, but it was nonetheless enough for me to get up and feel reenergized. Studies have shown that even a 15 minute nap can be enough to make you feel more revitalized.

You need to find out when you are at your most productive state. I slowly discovered throughout highschool that I worked best at night or at least the very late evening. Going to bed at 1 or 2 am was not uncommon during school nights, but this was fine for me because I would make up the hours by napping once I came home. Although it was hard to adjust to such a schedule I eventually made it routine. I enjoyed working at night because there was an added element of urgency and there was little room to procrastinate. Working under pressure is not for everyone, so you need to figure out what works best for you.

As an IB student you also need to learn to get sleep wherever and whenever you can. My bus ride to school took around an hour. I made sure that unless I had a test to study for or an assignment to complete I would try to sleep for most of that hour. Other classmates of mine would bring their own pillows and politely ask to nap during 'free periods' and sometimes this was permitted by the teacher. Those who pulled all-nighters would even try to nap during lunchtime after having something to eat.

Sleep is essential to being productive and motivated. A lack of sleep can result in careless errors in assignments and missing essential information in class. For the 16-18 year old age group, the recommended amount of sleep is usually quoted as 6-8 hours. If you are getting less than 5 hours on a regular basis then there might be cause for alarm. Remember that although this is only a two-year programme, you could potentially be doing more long-term damage to your health by missing out on sleep.

Second-hand Stress

It is often said that being surrounded by negative people can be contagious. The same is true for stress. If you surround yourself with students that constantly complain about the workload and the pressure then you are more likely to succumb to their state. Make sure you have plenty of people to talk to that are on top of their work – this will also incentivize you to work harder and be more efficient.

Although you may think that by surrounding yourself with students who are behind on their work and always worrying will somehow make you feel better about your own situation, this is usually not the case. These people will make you worry more. You need to avoid this second-hand stress at all costs.

PAST PAPERS

I'm sorry to disappoint you but if you have come here looking for free past papers and markschemes you are out of luck. At the same time, I wish to congratulate you because that kind of "I-need-past-papers" mentality is exactly what you need. If you have flipped through to this chapter in hopes of finding out where to get past papers and how to use them, then you can pat yourself on the back because you are now one step closer to getting 7's in your subjects.

If you have been reading this guide carefully then you should know just how much I have stressed the importance of past papers. Let me put it to you this way. If Internal Assessment takes around 25% of final IB grade, then your experience and practice with past papers could determine around half of what your final IB grade will be. The remaining 25% is down to a mixture of determination, natural academic ability and luck. Past papers are everything when it comes to acing your examinations.

Once again to truly understand the power of past papers, we need to think logically. The syllabuses for most subjects have been written many years ago. The IB examinations are written to test your knowledge and grasp of the syllabus material. Thus, there is only so much that they can possibly ask. If you look through past papers over and over again you are bound to see major similarities. Once again, the degree of similarity will vary across subjects, but nonetheless it is a fair generalisation. Think of it this way: there is a set amount of information you need to learn and the IBO wants to test your knowledge with respect to this information. Every year they will ask questions to test this knowledge. Surely there are only so many different ways they can test you. Eventually they start to run out of original questions.

Luckily for you, this has already happened. Look at the grade above you; they arguably were worse off. Similarly, the grade below you is better off. Why? Because yet another year of modern IB examinations has gone by. That means another set of past paper questions and markschemes has been made available. Consider yourself lucky that you have so much access to past papers and markschemes because 10 years ago this was certainly not the case.

At the top major UK universities (including Oxford and Cambridge) you will find it impossible to get your hands on any markschemes. Past examinations are usually available (and even that can be a hassle), but markschemes are non-existent. The reasoning for this is quite simple to understand. The universities don't want students to simply digest the markschemes without learning the material properly. It levels out the playing field and makes the competition for top marks fiercer. Luckily for you the IB does not have this policy. Past papers and markschemes are recommended by the IBO and made available – albeit at a small monetary cost.

Where do I get them?

The simple answer to this is anywhere you can. If you are amongst the lucky ones then it can be the case that your school has an abundance of money and resources and will readily supply you with past papers and markschemes because they know how valuable they are. On the other hand, you may be at a school that lacks the financial muscle to buy these for students and is honest enough to not photocopy any. Nonetheless the first place you need to go to is your school. Your teachers, the library, your IB coordinator – basically anyone that might be able to help you. At some schools students have access to nearly all available past examinations however the teachers may restrict what they give out because they may use them as future mock examinations. Even if the papers are covered in cobwebs and in a dusty old closet, make sure to get them out and look for more.

If that route fails your next best option would probably be to go to the one place that has the answers to almost everything; the Internet. Be aware that there are several problems with this approach. First of all the IB strictly forbids any independent persons to host past papers and markschemes on the internet and they regularly hunt down and threaten anyone who doesn't follow these rules. If you are lucky enough to find a website that does host past papers then it's unlikely to be there in a few weeks time. Also, the chances that all your subjects are there is very rare. Personally I have seen many websites over the years host past papers for free – most of which are now shut down.

The last option you have is definitely the most hassle-free: buying past papers and markschemes directly from the IBO website. Now don't get me wrong. I am against spending any more money on what is already a very expensive program. Nor do I understand why the IB would charge students more for additional "information." There seems to be an injustice because richer schools and families can afford to spend more on these papers putting the poorer candidates at a disadvantage. In fact, I have tried to petition the IBO to provide the papers freely for these exact reasons; however they argued that they had some sort of copyright obligation with the writers of the papers. They said they would take my points into consideration for the future. Nonetheless, one should consider these papers as an investment just like any other textbook or study guide.

What I strongly recommend you do is round up ten or so classmates that are interested in getting past papers and markschemes for a particular subject. If each of you chips in then together you can buy a copy off the IBO website. Once you have all the papers you need you can share the papers between each other because they will be made available in a downloadable pdf format. Additionally, once you're done with your exams you can sell the papers off to the grade below.

All in all you should never be spending any more money on past papers then you would on a textbook – and past papers are far more valuable than any textbook. You need to get your hands on these papers, one way or another.

How many?

Although I usually urge you do more past papers in rough rather than one or two thoroughly, this approach also has its limitations. A good general approximate that I recommend is doing at least 5 years worth of examinations (both May and November papers). This adds up to 10 separate examinations – which is a considerable amount of practice. Of course this will vary from subject to subject. For example for Group 1 topics, there is very little point in looking at more than 3 years worth of exams whereas for Mathematics HL you wouldn't do yourself any harm working through 10 years of examinations if you really want that 7. A good rule to follow is to make sure you do enough past papers so that you start seeing repeat questions. Only then will you become comfortable and familiar with what the questions ask you to do.

Also avoid going too far back into the database if you know there has been a serious change in syllabus/exam structure. For example, the Economics HL Paper 1 exam used to be multiple choice questions until several years back. There is little point in looking at too many of those multiple choice papers because you no longer have to sit such a paper. That being said, just because there has been a slight change in method of examination doesn't mean you should ignore the papers totally. For example, although you are no longer permitted a calculator in Mathematics Paper 1, looking at past Paper 1s could still help you prepare for Paper 2.

There are few feelings worse than having just sat an exam where one of the questions was incredibly similar to a past paper that you decided not to do. I highly doubt you can feel overly confident going into an examination if you haven't taken your chance to do all the past papers you could get your hands on (or at least glance over them properly). Make sure you don't have this regret – do enough past papers.

Past Papers vs. Markschemes

Some of you may be asking what's more important, the past paper or the markscheme? They are both of equal importance and you can't really have one without the other. There is no point in running through paper after paper if you have no way to check if your answers are even remotely correct. Similarly, you cannot just flick through random answers in the markschemes if you have no idea what the question was asking (unless, that is, the markscheme has the questions included).

Ultimately, you need to have both the past paper **and** the markscheme for every examination that you are interested in. You will undoubtedly spend more time with the markscheme than you will with the past paper because you will want to see exactly what examiners are looking for. Nonetheless, get the past papers as well in case you want to do a practice examination or want to get a "feel" for the structure of the exam.

How do I "do" the past paper?

Contrary to what your teachers may have told you, it is not a crime to have the markscheme with you whilst you are answering questions from a past paper. This is one of the best forms of revision and is a method that is severely underused by students.

Ideally, you would want to complete each paper properly in the time set and only then get out the markscheme to see what mistakes you made. But we don't live in an ideal world. You don't have the time to sit 3-hour mock examinations for hundreds of papers in 6 different subjects and then go through each one with the markscheme. Your revision doesn't even really start until all the assessment is sent off so you will at best have a month or two of pure revision.

So what's the best thing to do once you have obtained the papers and the markschemes? Well, it will largely depend on you and what works for you individually. Personally, I found that for subjects such as Economics and Geography, I needed the markscheme near me as I was answering the questions from the past papers. I would have a scrap piece of paper next to me as well, glance at the question, jot down a rough answer, and then check with the markscheme what I missed out.

For Mathematics and Physics however, I found that by looking at the answers before I fully finished the question I was cheating myself. As a result I usually kept the markscheme away until I was totally stumped or found some sort of answer. The key thing to keep in mind is that you need to be constantly writing. Don't fool yourself into thinking you can go and lie down on your couch, past paper in one hand, markscheme in the other. Your revision needs to be active.

From my experience, I found that writing bullet-point scrap answers for past paper questions helped me learn the material much more than simply pondering over the answer and glancing at the markscheme. Remember what you are ultimately aiming for: to understand the material and be able to answer the question to the examiner's expectations. Your work with past papers and markschemes should make you feel more confident. If you pick up a past paper and are in total fear of what they ask then clearly you are not yet prepared.

Don't underestimate the power of this technique. Markschemes are everything when it comes to scoring 7's in your subjects. Not only do they provide model answers but there is also a clear breakdown for the examiners for when to award marks. You have at your disposal everything that makes for a perfect examination answer. The closer you get to this perfection, the closer you will get to that 7. You will learn what it takes to make your paper worthy of a high mark. Learn to speak the examiner's lingo. Look for key words and phrases, memorize certain model definitions, and learn to give them what they are looking for.

By the time I was midway through my exams I had past papers and markschemes all over the place along with the model answers I wrote myself. The coffee table, the bedroom, the bathroom, the kitchen – everything and everywhere was covered with past papers. When you surround yourself with this information, you are less likely to forget it. By constantly consulting the past papers and markschemes you ensure that you will not be surprised by anything that could come up in the real examination.

SL/HL

Some of you may wonder whether there is any sense in going through past papers at a level which you do not necessarily do. This is at times fine if you are a Higher Level student looking to get a greater grasp of the questions and the syllabus, but I would not recommend that you go through Higher Level papers if you are a Standard Level student. You will not be "challenging yourself". You will probably just get confused and frightened because you won't be able to answer most of the questions. For example, I avoided looking at HL Physics papers because I found the SL ones challenging and adequate enough. That being said, I got too familiar with most of the HL Geography papers available so I started to go over a few SL papers (which was ok because the gap between SL and HL was not that great). Use your common sense and don't waste your time doing papers that are of no use to you.

IB Questionbank

The point of this chapter was to make you appreciate the potential that past papers and markschemes have to offer. The most successful IB candidates nowadays heavily rely on past examination questions simply because it is an unbeatable strategy. Your teachers will probably disagree that learning off past papers and markschemes is a more effective study technique than learning from textbooks/notes but they have not done the exams themselves. Trust me on this one. Unless you have done absolutely as many past papers as you possibly can you will not be ready to sit the examinations and get that grade 7. I cannot stress this enough but I trust you have enough good judgement to see the logic behind this.

EXAMINATION TECHNIQUE

Although you should keep in mind that you need specific revision techniques for each individual subject, there remains much to be said about examination technique in general. Your success in the exams will not only rely on how well prepared you are in terms of material, but also how well you perform under pressure. To deal with this you will need to master a few exam techniques. Most of them are simple, but nonetheless often forgotten or severely underestimated.

Time Management

You need to be able to allocate your time proportionally across the entire duration of the exam. This includes taking off a few minutes from the beginning for reading and the end for proofreading. Whatever time you devote to actual writing and working out should be spaced out across the whole exam. Luckily, the IB have made your task even simpler as they now indicate how many points each question and sub-question is worth. For most papers this is the same year in year out; however pay close attention to this as it will decide how many minutes you will need to spend on the question. If it takes you less time to answer than you had anticipated then move on to next question as you may need that extra time.

You absolutely must, and under no exceptions, finish your exam from beginning to end. If you have not answered all the questions that were required of you then you can consider your grade 7 a missed opportunity. Once the examiner sees that you have left questions at the end blank, this immediately sends out a signal that you have mismanaged your time. This mistake is made every year by countless numbers of bright students and the only reason for it is poor organization and time use – something that is not expected from the best candidates.

There is absolutely no reason why you should not have enough time to finish the exam. I hear this excuse all the time but the truth is you *did* have enough time, you just didn't use it wisely. It's one thing to leave a question blank because you just had no idea how to answer it – which is something I also highly discourage. But it's a totally different matter if you didn't answer the last few questions because you messed up your timing.

Command Terms

These 'command terms' are specific words and phrases that the IB likes to use in their exam questions. The IB examiners are not just trying to grade you on your knowledge of the subject, but they want to test your ability to actually answer the question that they have set out for you.

This is not something that is unique to the IB examinations. At university, and also in some job applications, you will be tested on your ability to really understand what is being asked. There is no point in answering *how* something happened if the question asked *why* it happened. Get used to reading questions carefully and answering accordingly because this is a skill that you will reuse often.

Again, your success at identifying and answering these command terms will largely depend on your practice with past papers. That being said, no amount of preparation can spare you from being careless. For this reason make sure to double-check what is being asked. If time is available then I even recommend you highlight or underline the command term so that you don't forget what it is you need to answer.

There's nothing worse than writing an answer *explaining* something when you were simply asked to *define* it.

Extra Materials

Along with your lucky charms and favourite pen I strongly advise that you bring in a well-functioning clock in order to be able to manage your time properly. This varies amongst personal taste but I know that some like to have wrist watches, while some bring digital clocks, and I have even seen some bring countdown timers that were pre-set to countdown the exam duration. You need to keep in mind that although there may already be a clock in the exam room you could be assigned a seat all the way in the back. Perhaps your eyesight isn't as great as you thought it was and as a result you struggle to see the time. Don't take any of these chances. Bring some sort of time device with you.

I always have a little bit of paranoia when it comes to calculators malfunctioning in exams so I strongly recommend that you bring a spare calculator (not necessarily the graphing one) or at least a spare set of batteries for the calculator-based exams. It goes without saying that you need a spare pen or two just in case the one you have runs out. Also try to bring a set of highlighters because you can use these to remind yourself of the key terms in a question as discussed later on in this chapter.

Answer the Question, Nothing but the Question

This is pretty self-explanatory. When answering any question on the IB exams you have to make sure you address the exact phrasing in the question and give the examiner exactly what he/she is looking for. For all of my examinations I brought along a highlighter or two so that I could highlight key words in the question sentence. For example, if a math question stated "give the answer in cm^3" I would highlight the cm^3 part. I know that this might sounds a little pointless and a waste of time but you would be surprised to see how many candidates "forget" certain parts of the question. One common example is when a question asks you to "explain why" and you write an excellent essay on "how". By highlighting the "explain why" part you will significantly narrow the chances of this kind of slip up.

There is usually absolutely no reason to write more than what is required. If the question is worth two marks this means the examiner is probably looking for two key points – no more, no less. You don't have time to be writing everything you know. You need to pick the most valuable bits of information and keep to your own time limit. There are no "bonus" points and you will not get extra credit for writing what is not required. Remember, the key is to write efficiently and aim for maximum marks with minimum nonsense.

Less is More – Usually

There are a few exceptions to the above. If, in the unlikely scenario that you stumble upon a question where you don't know how to *fully* answer then sometimes writing *everything* you do know on the topic *might* give you a few more marks. This technique is very beneficial if used wisely, but it can also be very risky and damaging to your time if you abuse it. I can give you a good example. Suppose you get a "define" question worth two marks. This usually means you need to give two concrete points in order to get full marks. Let's suppose that you could only remember one. Whereas normally I would suggest that you not waste your time and just move onto the next question, there will be times when a little bit more 'filler' just might get you that other mark. Either expand on your first point or throw in some other information that could, *maybe*, give you the remaining marks.

Remember that directly you will not get marked down for writing more. Indirectly, you always run the risk of losing valuable time. There is a general belief that examiners will only read the first few points you make and ignore the rest if you haven't hit the nail on the head yet. Personally I find that this notion is too general to apply to every examiner in every subject. Your best bet is to keep writing "educated guesses" until you think you have pretty good odds at getting most of the marks. You won't lose marks, but you might not gain any either. Remember that you are facing a balancing act – writing more BS versus having more time to answer later questions.

Give Yourself Space

One of the first things you should do when you sit at your desk is carefully lay out all of your materials. You don't want to be doing a three hour examination curled up uncomfortably on a tiny working space. Place the examination paper on one side and the fill-in answer booklet next to it. Arrange your pencil case and all of your materials somewhere neatly in the corner. Make sure that your workspace is not one giant mess or else this could reflect negatively on your answers.

Start with What you Know

If the exam is parts-based then I highly advise you to start with the parts where you are most comfortable and ones that you find most enjoyable. Not only will this ensure that you not waste time attempting trickier questions but you will also feel more confident and optimistic knowing that you have already answered many correct answers. There is no strict rule governing where you need to start and finish your section-based exam so don't treat it in a strictly chronological order. Do what you feel happier doing first and leave the trickier bits for later.

Handwriting

Do you have handwriting that needs its own Rosetta Stone? If so, you need to make at least some effort to improve it or else you risk having your paper deciphered angrily and possibly downgraded. I highly suggest that when you are doing past papers in your revision, you start to focus also on the neatness of your handwriting. I personally haven't heard of any cases where a student's paper was simply illegible, but I am sure that they exist. If you find that your writing speed is significantly slower, then you might be better off not bothering with drastically improving your handwriting. If your teachers need to constantly remind you to write neater then please do pay attention. Nothing is more frustrating to an examiner then to decode your cluttered calligraphy.

Leaving Early?

There are very few things in the world that frustrate and anger me more than seeing candidates get up and leave examinations with plenty of time to spare. You are given the time limit for a reason – use it! You have to be incredibly stupid to give up and just leave the exam with an hour to spare. There is absolutely no reason – none whatsoever – for you to leave before the time is up. Don't think you can just cross your arms on your desk and put your head down for a nap either. That would be equally retarded. I don't care whether you think you have answered all the questions and proofread enough. Unless you are 100% confident that you got 100% don't even consider leaving early. And no, you're not "cool" or "rebellious" for leaving with time to spare.

Proofreading

You absolutely must make sure you leave a few minutes at the end of your examination for proofreading. This is more important in non-essay based exams such as Mathematics and Group 4 subjects. Even in examinations for Economics, going back and making sure your diagrams are properly labelled could score you a few extra points. I'm not suggesting you make sure that you crossed all your t's and dotted all of your i's but at least make sure the majority of the exam is legible and that you avoided any silly mistakes. The few marks that you pick up when proofreading could prove vital if you're on the edge between two distinct marks. You will lose and gain most of your marks in the beginning and at the end of your examination – so make sure you make a positive start and always go back and proofread at the end.

Ignoring Distractions

Although the exams are supposed to happen in complete silence there may be times when distractions are simply inevitable. For example the kid sitting next to you who has never heard of cough medicine and is having non-stop bronchitis-like coughing. Or the student who accidently drops his pencil only for it to roll all the way across the room. I remember for one of my first Mathematics exams the weather in the morning was terrible. It was hailing, raining and thundering all at once. The fact that our examination centre had a semi-glass ceiling provided very surreal Dolby-digital surround sound. It was probably the most frustrating thing to encounter when you are trying to focus on a HL Mathematics paper. If you don't mind wearing them, bringing some ear plugs is also a viable solution – although make sure you get this approved by the invigilators beforehand.

You need to teach yourself how to work around distractions. Don't become frustrated and punch the desk. Nor should you start to complain and lash out on your examination co-ordinator for having so many distractions. Just sit your exam and focus on what's in front of you. Do whatever you need to do in order to clear your head and relax.

APPEALS/RETAKES

Once you receive your examination results in early June one of three things will happen. You may get the grades you were expecting and get what was required for your university. In this ideal scenario your IB adventure is over, and you can finally move on. Alternatively, you may receive your results and find out that you *deservedly* fell short in a subject or two, or perhaps failed something, and as a result your first choice university offer is no longer an option. The final scenario is that you receive your results and find that there are a few subjects where you know you should have done better. You are shocked because, as things stand, you cannot get into your first choice university or perhaps even your backup choice. There are several options that you may choose to take, outlined below.

Appealing

I'll be honest with you. When I first got my IB results in June, I did not get into my first university of choice. I got 42 points but fell short in HL Mathematics because I got a 6 instead of the required 7. My offer from Oxford was 40+ points overall, with 7s in HL Mathematics and HL Economics. I wasn't too surprised because I knew if there was one subject where I might fall short, it was definitely maths. Nonetheless, as things stood, I was not going to get a place at Oxford. I called up my coordinator and told him the situation. He highly recommended I appeal not just the mathematics grade, but also the 6's I got in SL English and SL Physics. The logic behind this was that if I didn't go up in maths, then at least maybe Oxford would reconsider if I got 43 or 44 points overall.

After several weeks I was informed that my English and Physics grades would not improve. This was very disappointing because I felt that my English exams went perfectly and I had superb IA marks for both English and Physics. I felt like there was no chance that my maths grade would increase because first of all I was predicted a 5, and second of all because maths is rather objective – there are right and wrong answers with little room for grey areas and errors by examiners. Well, I was mistaken. I received the news from my coordinator that the grade had gone up to a 7, so I had met my offer and got a total of 43 points.

In recent years the IB has adjusted its appeal policy and you now risk being *downgraded* if the remarked work is of a lower score than the initial mark. This makes the decision to appeal a lot more difficult. You need to be honest with yourself and consult your IB coordinator before taking any action. Of course any appeal process will come at a financial cost, but I would say that if it is affecting your future then the financial cost is worth it. Besides, if the grade does change you will be refunded the full amount. Would I have appealed if I got my first choice of university and could see no direct benefit of a higher IB score? Probably not. I would recommend appealing only if it will affect your university decision.

Retakes

In the unlikely scenario that you completely mess up your IB exams there is always the option of re-taking them in November. I am not a big fan of this option for several reasons. First of all, re-taking in the winter exam session still means that you will miss out on a year of university unless you can find somewhere that starts after the winter break. If not, you would be better off repeating the year and sitting the examinations in May.

Second of all, re-taking exams is only a good option if you genuinely think that things will change. There is no point in redoing the exams if your approach is the same. If something tragic happened that distracted you from performing at your best level, then retakes can be a good opportunity for a second chance. If, however, you failed to meet your targets because you did not prepare adequately, then chances are this will happen again during retakes.

For these reasons retakes should only be considered as the final resort. It goes without saying that if you missed a university offer by a small amount then you should first appeal your grades before you even consider retaking the exam.

ACADEMIC DISHONESTY

If you have come here looking for ways to cheat on your exams then you are out of luck. It's not that I'm an extremely honourable and moral person (although I would like to think so) it's just that there is no point in cheating. The information I have provided so far in this book *is* in a way tricking the system without *actually* cheating. So you are technically not doing anything wrong, you are just taking advantage of certain aspects in order to get a higher grade – something that any clever student would do naturally. It is one thing to plagiarize your essay, but it's a completely different matter to slightly "manipulate" your lab report data in order to get higher marks. This chapter won't give you the best tips on how to cheat. In fact it will do quite the opposite – it will tell you why most methods of cheating fail and what the consequences usually mean.

You have to be pretty stupid to follow a two year program only to then have your diploma taken away for academic malpractice. That's two year of your life practically wasted. If you fail the IB diploma because of cheating then you are pretty much screwed. Why risk two whole years of relatively demanding work so that you can bump your grade up a little bit? The risk is simply not worth the reward. It's even more redundant given that you can easily get a higher grade by simply following the guidelines set out in this book. No matter who you are, there is absolutely no reason for you to even think about cheating.

Although the IB originated in Switzerland, don't expect them to be very understanding, or "neutral" towards cheating. Any form of academic dishonesty is dealt with the upmost seriousness. The vast majority of the time when you are caught and reported you will lose your diploma. Not only does cheating carry serious risks but you will also put yourself under more pressure. The threat of being caught will make you underperform and provide an unnecessary distraction.

Plagiarism

Plagiarizing is probably the most common type of academic dishonesty found in the IB program. I'm not going to go into an in-depth discussion of what constitutes as plagiarism and how to properly source – your school should have that already shoved down your throat. I merely want to explain to you what happens when you try to do it. Hopefully this way you will avoid "accidently" doing it and think twice before you complete any piece of work for the IB.

Many of you may have heard of the website TurnItIn.com. This website scans for plagiarism. Depending on what school you are in, you may have it that your teachers scan every single piece of work that you hand in electronically. For those of you that have no idea what I'm talking about let me explain. Turnitin.com (amongst many other more sophisticated websites) scans documents for any evidence of plagiarism. They take your words and check them across a multitude of sources: websites, paid websites, written books, magazines, journals, etc. The program then composes a very in-depth report that specifies exactly how much of your document is plagiarized and to what degree.

These expensive plagiarism scanners that the IB uses are growing in sophistication every year. Almost every possible essay-writing database is now listed, along with written books that have been made into e-books. Even if you paid ridiculous money for someone to custom write your Extended Essay, chances are the scanners at turnitin.com will catch it because they can afford to scan almost every database.

So what does all of this mean for you? This should be a wakeup call for those of you who are likely to plagiarize "unintentionally." I'm talking about those of you who thought it was ok to throw in a few sentences here and there from your textbook because it's not available online. Almost everything is now available online and turnitin.com will scan these archives.

The consequences of plagiarism will more than likely lead to you failing that specific piece of work, and, depending on the degree of plagiarism, maybe even your entire diploma. I trust that you realise the dishonest aspect of plagiarism and will refrain from trying. More importantly however, I want to warn you to make sure that you don't accidently and unintentionally plagiarize either. I know that sentence doesn't make much sense, but it's for your own good that you make sure that none of your work is anyone else's words. So please, think twice before you include any sentence or idea that is clearly not your own (without proper citation).

Cheating on Exam Day

Why in the world would you even contemplate cheating on the actual IB exam day? If you're at a respectable and honest IB school then chances are that your exam centre is going to have some of the most vigilant proctors making sure that your every breath and sneeze is natural. You and your fellow candidates are going to be like little sheep surrounded by a pack of wolves.

Even before you walk into the exam room your face will tell the whole story. Even the bravest of you that lack any conscience will struggle to conceal that nervous and tense look when you step into the room. Chances are that even before you actually begin to cheat you will get caught cheating. This paragraph (and probably chapter) only applies to a small proportion of candidates out there, but nonetheless it's important to get the message out there that cheating on the exams is near impossible – and stupid.

Almost anything you can think of has already been taken into account. Random pre-exam calculator checks, plastic see-though bags, no talking in the exam centre, assisted toilet breaks, only bottled water. For every cheating method there is already an answer. The only "cheating" left for you to do is to follow the legitimate advice and tips that I have been suggesting. On exam day the only thing you should be thinking of is the exam itself. Anything else on your mind will distract you from doing your best. The IB diploma is not some middle school exam where you can write the answers on the palm of your hand, or slip in a cheat sheet. This is one of the most prestigious and respected high school programs in the world and they are not about to let their reputation slip as a result of academic malpractice.

As long as we are on the subject of cheating, there is one final word of warning. With the recent rise in cell phone and internet use, it has become almost inevitable that students discuss exam questions and answers online and over the phone. Make sure you are not amongst them. Schools have begun paying incredible attention to this and I have heard of cases where students were tracked through Facebook or their cell phone and eventually stripped of their diploma because they broke several rules about revealing exam details before the examinations were completed worldwide.

Given that the IB is an international program there are small possibilities for the manipulation of time zones in order to get exam information. But again let me warn you. Schools have begun to monitor students' cell phone use before and after the examinations. Also more and more papers are being divided into several time zones. There's probably nothing worse than being fully ready for an examination only to turn the paper over and realise you have crammed the last hour on questions that are not there. Also, if you are ever asked for question details from a friend living in the far west then please ignore them. Why would you want to make the same exam easier for someone else when at the end of the day you are going to be judged and graded in a somewhat standardized way? You are competing against other IB schools so don't put yourself at a disadvantage.

The message here is pretty crystal clear: don't even try to cheat during your IB program because you will more than likely get caught and there is very little benefit. You can achieve amazing results without needing to plagiarize or be dishonest. Getting caught cheating will have severe repercussions for you later on in life. You can forget about going to any respectable university if your diploma is taken away because of academic dishonesty. Not only is it a burden on your academic future but it also has serious social and familial consequences.